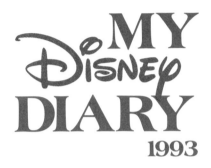

MY DISNEY DIARY
1993

MY DISNEY DIARY 1993

Grolier Enterprises Corp.

STAFF
Fern L. Mamberg   *Executive Editor*
Michèle A. McLean   *Art Director*
Walter Dalia   *Production Manager*

MY Disney DIARY

*As you can plainly see,
it's 1993.
So start to plan the year
with your Disney Diary!*

Your Disney Diary has a special page for each of the 52 weeks in 1993. You can write down all the wonderful things you are looking forward to. Write down the birthdays of your family and friends—and don't forget your own birthday! Mark down parties and holidays. Write down when your vacation starts. And as things happen—fun things, happy things, strange things, surprising things, any kind of thing—write them down in your Diary, too.

Talking about fun things, your Diary is full of them. There are puzzles and poems and games and gags. Stories to read? Ideas for things to make and do? They're also in your Diary.

When the year is over, hold on to your Diary. Save it as a memory book. It will be great fun to look back on all the good times you had in 1993.

JANUARY
THE FIRST MONTH

January 1 is the first day of 1993. So say "Happy New Year!" to your family and friends. And you have a good year too!

What will you do on New Year's Day? It's a legal holiday, and schools are closed. You'll have plenty of time to visit friends. Maybe one of them is having a New Year's Day party. You can talk about your New Year's resolutions—promises to do better in the coming year. What are your New Year's resolutions for 1993?

In the northern part of the world, January is the heart of winter. The wind blows hard, and it can be icy cold. There may even be snow on the ground. If there is, you'll have lots of fun. Get out your sled and go sledding. Build a snowman or a snow castle. Go ice skating. Have a friendly snowball fight. Just make sure that you bundle up and keep warm!

Special Days of Winter

Days I'm looking forward to from January to March:

_____

_____

_____

Birthdays: _____

Holidays: _____

Special days or vacations: _____

_____

DECEMBER 28, 1992 TO JANUARY 3, 1993

MONDAY

28

DECEMBER

TUESDAY

29

DECEMBER

WEDNESDAY

30

DECEMBER

THURSDAY

31

DECEMBER

FRIDAY

1

JANUARY

New Year's Day

SATURDAY

2

JANUARY

SUNDAY

3

JANUARY

MONDAY

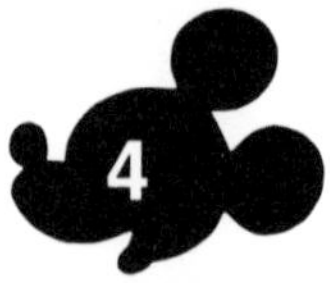

4

JANUARY

TUESDAY

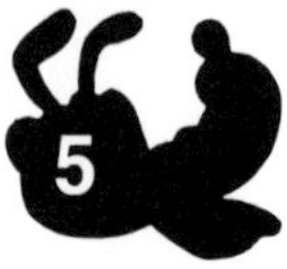

5

JANUARY

WEDNESDAY

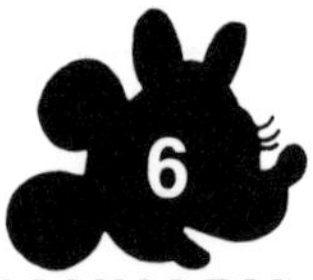

6

JANUARY

THURSDAY

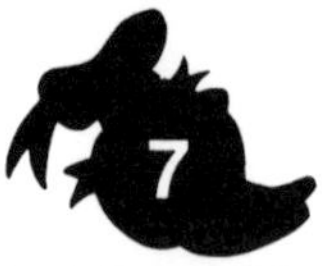

7

JANUARY

FRIDAY

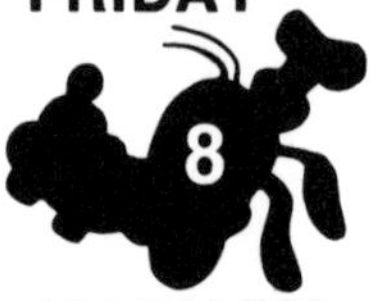

8

JANUARY

SATURDAY

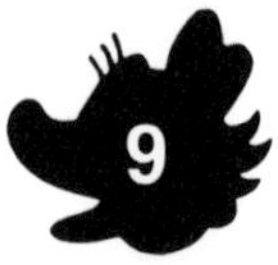

9

JANUARY

SUNDAY

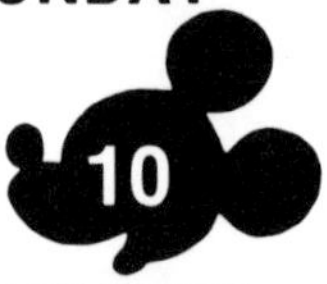

10

JANUARY

This Is Me

It's fun to write down important facts about yourself. Fill in the blanks below. Ask your parents to help you if you don't know some of these things.

Name: _____

Weight: _____

Birth Date: _____

Shoe Size: _____

Height: _____

Shirt Size: _____

Brothers/Sisters (Name and Birth Date): _____

_____

_____

Look in the mirror till you're sure you know just what you look like. Then draw a picture of yourself on a piece of paper. Do you look like your photo?

Paste a
photo
of yourself
here.

MONDAY

11

JANUARY

TUESDAY

12

JANUARY

WEDNESDAY

13

JANUARY

THURSDAY

14

JANUARY

FRIDAY

15

JANUARY

SATURDAY

16

JANUARY

SUNDAY

17

JANUARY

UP, UP, AND AWAY....

Have you ever watched a balloon gently rise into the sky and wished that you could float into the heavens, too? People have been taking balloon flights for a long time. Of course, they don't use the small balloons you hold onto with a string. They use big hot-air balloons.

In a hot-air balloon, passengers ride beneath the balloon in a jumbo basket. Also in the basket is the burner, which sends hot air up into the balloon. Hot air is lighter than cold air, so it rises. And when the hot air in the balloon rises, it carries the balloon with it.

The first living creatures to make a balloon flight were a sheep, a duck, and a rooster. This flight took place in France in 1783. Soon people were riding in balloons, too. And ten years later, on January 9, 1793, Jean Pierre Blanchard became the first person to make a balloon flight in the United States. So this year, 1993, is the 200th anniversary of ballooning in America.

MONDAY

18

JANUARY

Martin Luther King Jr. Day

TUESDAY

19

JANUARY

WEDNESDAY

20

JANUARY

THURSDAY

21

JANUARY

FRIDAY

22

JANUARY

SATURDAY

23

JANUARY

SUNDAY

24

JANUARY

JANUARY 25 TO JANUARY 31

MONDAY

25

JANUARY

TUESDAY

26

JANUARY

WEDNESDAY

27

JANUARY

THURSDAY

28

JANUARY

FRIDAY

29

JANUARY

SATURDAY

30

JANUARY

SUNDAY

31

JANUARY

FEBRUARY
THE SECOND MONTH

February has 28 days. Every other month has 30 or 31 days. So February is the shortest month of the year. And it's one of the coldest months in the northern part of the world. But don't worry! It's the last full month of winter. February 2 is Groundhog Day. According to an old legend, that's the day the groundhog, or woodchuck, is supposed to wake up from its long winter sleep. And if this furry little animal doesn't see its shadow, spring is right around the corner.

February 14 is Valentine's Day, which is one of the happiest holidays of the year. You can give Valentine cards to all the people you love.

George Washington and Abraham Lincoln, two great American presidents, were born in February. Their birthdays are celebrated together on the third Monday of February. This holiday is known as Presidents' Day.

MONDAY

1

FEBRUARY

TUESDAY

2

FEBRUARY

Groundhog Day

WEDNESDAY

3

FEBRUARY

THURSDAY

4

FEBRUARY

FRIDAY

5

FEBRUARY

SATURDAY

6

FEBRUARY

SUNDAY

7

FEBRUARY

It's great fun to watch your shadow, no matter where you roam;
that's what Robert Louis Stevenson did before he wrote this poem.

MY SHADOW

I have a little shadow that goes
    in and out with me,
And what can be the use of him
    is more than I can see.
He is very, very like me from
    the heels up to the head;
And I see him jump before me,
    when I jump into my bed.

The funniest thing about him
    is the way he likes to grow—
Not at all like proper children,
    which is always very slow;
For he sometimes shoots up taller
    like an india-rubber ball,
And he sometimes gets so little
    that there's none of him at all.

He hasn't got a notion of how
    children ought to play,
And can only make a fool of me in
    every sort of way.
He stays so close beside me, he's
    a coward you can see;
I'd think shame to stick to nurse
    as that shadow sticks to me!

One morning, very early, before
    the sun was up,
I rose and found the shining dew
    on every buttercup;
But my lazy little shadow, like
    an arrant sleepy-head,
Had stayed at home behind me
    and was fast asleep in bed.

FEBRUARY 8 TO FEBRUARY 14

MONDAY

8

FEBRUARY

TUESDAY

9

FEBRUARY

WEDNESDAY

10

FEBRUARY

THURSDAY

11

FEBRUARY

FRIDAY

12

FEBRUARY

Abraham Lincoln was born in 1809

SATURDAY

13

FEBRUARY

SUNDAY

14

FEBRUARY

Valentine's Day

ARIEL'S VALENTINE

Ariel wants to give a valentine to Prince Eric. Can you help her find the way? Start under the sea and work your way to the surface.

A Frosted Fairyland

Did you ever wake up on a cold morning to find the world looking like a glittering wonderland? Did diamonds seem to sparkle on all the plant life right outside your door? The sparkles weren't diamonds, of course. They were frost—which formed overnight while you slept.

Frost forms in much the same way as dew. During the day, sunlight warms everything it touches—tree branches, leaves, stones. At night, these objects

begin to cool off. When they are cool enough, water vapor in the air condenses on them. The vapor forms tiny droplets. This is dew. But if the surfaces of the objects cool to freezing or below, the water vapor changes to crystals of ice. This is frost.

The early morning sun reveals the frosted fairyland—the twigs and branches in their armor of ice, and the bright berries that seem to have been dipped in sparkling sugar.

FEBRUARY 15 TO FEBRUARY 21

MONDAY

15

FEBRUARY

Presidents' Day

TUESDAY

16

FEBRUARY

WEDNESDAY

17

FEBRUARY

THURSDAY

18

FEBRUARY

FRIDAY

19

FEBRUARY

SATURDAY

20

FEBRUARY

SUNDAY

21

FEBRUARY

FEBRUARY 22 TO FEBRUARY 28

MONDAY

22

FEBRUARY

George Washington was born in 1732

TUESDAY

23

FEBRUARY

WEDNESDAY

24

FEBRUARY

Ash Wednesday

THURSDAY

25

FEBRUARY

FRIDAY

26

FEBRUARY

SATURDAY

27

FEBRUARY

SUNDAY

28

FEBRUARY

Joke Time

Why do bees hum?
Because they know the tune but not the words!

What did the beach say as the tide came in?
Long time no sea!

BABY CELERY: "Mama, where did I come from?"
MOTHER CELERY: "Hush, dear. The stalk brought you."

How can you catch a rabbit?
Hide behind a bush and make a noise like a carrot!

MARCH
THE THIRD MONTH

In the northern part of the world, the beginning of March can be as wintry as January or February. It's often cold and very windy. And lots of snow can fall. More than a hundred years ago, one early March storm dumped more than four feet of snow on the eastern part of the United States. People still talk about this Blizzard of 1888.

But spring arrives toward the end of the month. The days become sunnier and warmer. Birds start flying north from their winter homes in the south. Chipmunks and other animals are getting ready to leave their winter dens.

It's also a time for celebrations. One of the grandest is St. Patrick's Day. On March 17, Irish people all over the world honor St. Patrick, the patron saint of Ireland, with lively parades and marching bands. You'll see many people wearing green that day—which is Ireland's national color.

MARCH 1 TO MARCH 7

MONDAY

1

MARCH

TUESDAY

2

MARCH

WEDNESDAY

3

MARCH

THURSDAY

4

MARCH

FRIDAY

5

MARCH

SATURDAY

6

MARCH

SUNDAY

7

MARCH

Basil's Secret Message

Basil, the Great Mouse Detective, is working on a hot case. And while tracking down the clues, he discovers something that's very important. He wants to tell his assistant, Dr. David Q. Dawson, what he has learned, so he writes it down in code.

In his code, every number stands for a letter. 1 stands for A, 2 stands for B, 3 stands for C, and so on. Decode this well-known saying—then try writing your own secret message for a friend to decode.

6·15·21·18 ✶ 5·25·5·19 ✶ 19·5·5 ✶ 13·15·18·5 ✶ 20·8·1·14 ✶ 20·23·15

What the secret message says: Four eyes see more than two.

MARCH 8 TO MARCH 14

MONDAY
8
MARCH

TUESDAY
9
MARCH

WEDNESDAY
10
MARCH

THURSDAY
11
MARCH

FRIDAY
12
MARCH

SATURDAY
13
MARCH

SUNDAY
14
MARCH

MONDAY

15

MARCH

TUESDAY

16

MARCH

WEDNESDAY

17

MARCH

St. Patrick's Day

THURSDAY

18

MARCH

FRIDAY

19

MARCH

SATURDAY

20

MARCH

Spring begins in the Northern Hemisphere
Fall begins in the Southern Hemisphere

SUNDAY

21

MARCH

Winter Memories

Write down the things you liked best this winter.

My happiest day: _____

My favorite television show: _____

The game I played most often: _____

The friend I had the most fun with: _____

My favorite book: _____

My nicest Valentine: _____

The best trip I took: _____

MARCH 22 TO MARCH 28

MONDAY

22

MARCH

TUESDAY

23

MARCH

WEDNESDAY

24

MARCH

THURSDAY

25

MARCH

FRIDAY

26

MARCH

SATURDAY

27

MARCH

SUNDAY

28

MARCH

APRIL
THE FOURTH MONTH

The animals that have slept all winter are fully awake now and are sniffing the warmer air. Birds are building nests and laying eggs. Trees are budding. Farmers are sowing their crops, and gardeners are planting flowers. And it's time for the first baseball game! It's April, the first full month of spring.

"April showers bring May flowers" is an old saying. And it's true that April is usually a very wet month. But the rain makes the flowers bloom and the grass green. All that rain may not make you happy. But be sure to keep a smile on your face on April 1! This is April Fools Day. You and your friends can have fun playing jokes on one another.

April is also a time of religious celebrations all over the world. Christians observe Easter. Jews observe Passover. And Buddhists celebrate Buddha's birthday.

MARCH 29 TO APRIL 4

MONDAY

29

MARCH

TUESDAY

30

MARCH

WEDNESDAY

31

MARCH

THURSDAY

1

APRIL

April Fools' Day

FRIDAY

2

APRIL

SATURDAY

3

APRIL

SUNDAY

4

APRIL

Palm Sunday

Daylight Savings Time begins
(set your clock ahead one hour)

Special Days of Spring

Days I'm looking forward to from April to June: _____

_____

_____

Birthdays: _____

Holidays: _____

Special days or vacations: _____

_____

_____

_____

_____

_____

_____

A Collection of Leaves

Do you live in an area where there are lots of different trees around? Do you love nature? If you've answered yes to both questions, you might be interested in a fascinating hobby—making a leaf collection.

If you want to keep leaves for a long time, you must press them. Start by picking some leaves that are in good condition. (Watch out for poison ivy!) Arrange the leaves on sheets of old newspaper so that they don't touch each other. Then cover them with more newspapers.

Put a board on top and weigh it down with heavy books. Change the newspapers every day. The leaves should be dry in about a week.

Place the dried leaves on sheets of heavy paper, one or two leaves to a sheet. Then fasten down the tips of the leaves and the stems with cellophane tape or white glue. Attach a label identifying the leaf and giving whatever other information you wish. You can keep the sheets in a loose-leaf binder or a scrapbook.

APRIL 5 TO APRIL 11

MONDAY

5

APRIL

TUESDAY

6

APRIL

Passover

WEDNESDAY

7

APRIL

THURSDAY

8

APRIL

FRIDAY

9

APRIL

Good Friday

SATURDAY

10

APRIL

SUNDAY

11

APRIL

Easter

APRIL 12 TO APRIL 18

MONDAY

12

APRIL

TUESDAY

13

APRIL

WEDNESDAY

14

APRIL

THURSDAY

15

APRIL

FRIDAY

16

APRIL

SATURDAY

17

APRIL

SUNDAY

18

APRIL

ANIMAL FATHERS

Many young animals need the care and protection of their mothers. Many need their fathers, too. Male wolves and male marmosets, a kind of monkey, are among those animals that help raise their young.

Male emperor penguins are also devoted animal fathers. They live in the frozen land of Antarctica, and their home is a giant sheet of ice. Emperor penguins can't build nests because there are no trees or other plants. So the males use their *feet* as nests. After the female lays an egg, the male places it on top of his webbed feet. There, it's covered and kept warm by a feathered flap that hangs down from his belly. When the egg hatches, the chick huddles between its father's feet. At last the mother takes over, and the father waddles off to the sea for a well-deserved meal—his first in months.

DINING OUT

Donald is treating Daisy to dinner in a fancy restaurant. They ordered big plates of spaghetti—and lots of other foods, too (listed below). Place the names of the foods in alphabetical order. Then write them in the word boxes. Read the circled letters. They spell Daisy's favorite fruit!

STEAK · FRANKFURTER · CABBAGE · YAMS · MACARONI · CREAM · SPINACH

Answers:

MONDAY

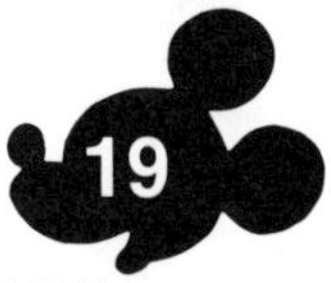

19

APRIL

TUESDAY

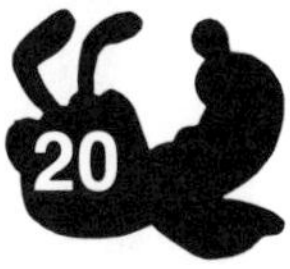

20

APRIL

WEDNESDAY

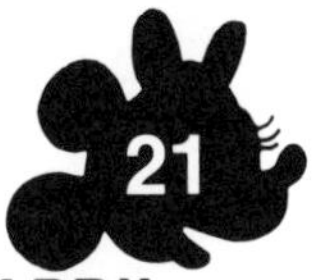

21

APRIL

THURSDAY

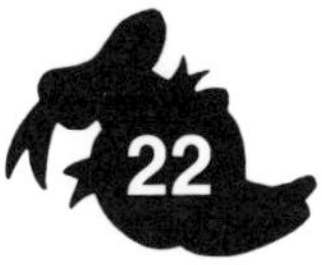

22

APRIL

FRIDAY

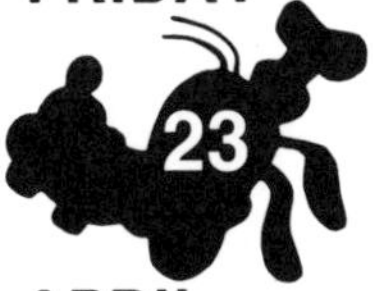

23

APRIL

SATURDAY

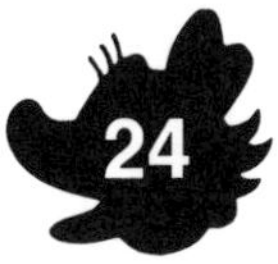

24

APRIL

SUNDAY

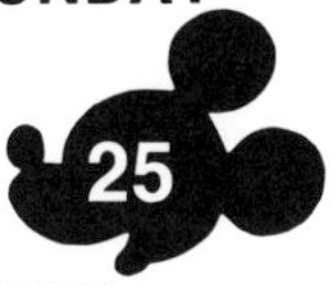

25

APRIL

MAY
THE FIFTH MONTH

"There are twelve months in all the year,
As I hear many men say,
But the merriest month in all the year
Is the merry month of May."

These lines are from a ballad about Robin Hood. And May truly is a beautiful month. The trees are in bloom, and colorful flowers are everywhere. The first day of May is called May Day, and in many places it's celebrated as a holiday. People dance around a maypole —a tall pole covered with colorful ribbons and flowers.

Mothers are especially merry in May, because Mother's Day is celebrated on the second Sunday of the month. Don't forget to tell your mother you love her.

The soldiers who have fought for the United States are also honored in May. Their special day—Memorial Day —falls on the last Monday of the month.

APRIL 26 TO MAY 2

MONDAY

26
APRIL

TUESDAY
27
APRIL

WEDNESDAY
28
APRIL

THURSDAY
29
APRIL

FRIDAY
30
APRIL

SATURDAY
1
MAY

May Day

SUNDAY
2
MAY

SAVE THE RAIN FOREST

The air is warm, damp, and heavy. There are so many trees and vines that you can't see very far. High above, monkeys chatter in the treetops. Snakes slither along the branches. Beautiful butterflies dart here and there. And bright red poisonous frogs hop along the ground. These are only a few of the nearly 2 million kinds of plants and animals that live in tropical rain forests.

Tropical rain forests cover a narrow band of Earth near the equator. They exist only in Africa, South and Central America, Asia, and Oceania. The world's biggest rain forest is around the Amazon River, in Brazil.

But the rain forests are disappearing. People are cutting down the trees for lumber. They are building farms, roads, and even cities there. And they are digging up minerals. In doing so, they are destroying tens of thousands of different kinds of animals and plants. It's hoped that the people of the world will find ways to save the rain forests before more living things are lost forever.

MAY 3 TO MAY 9

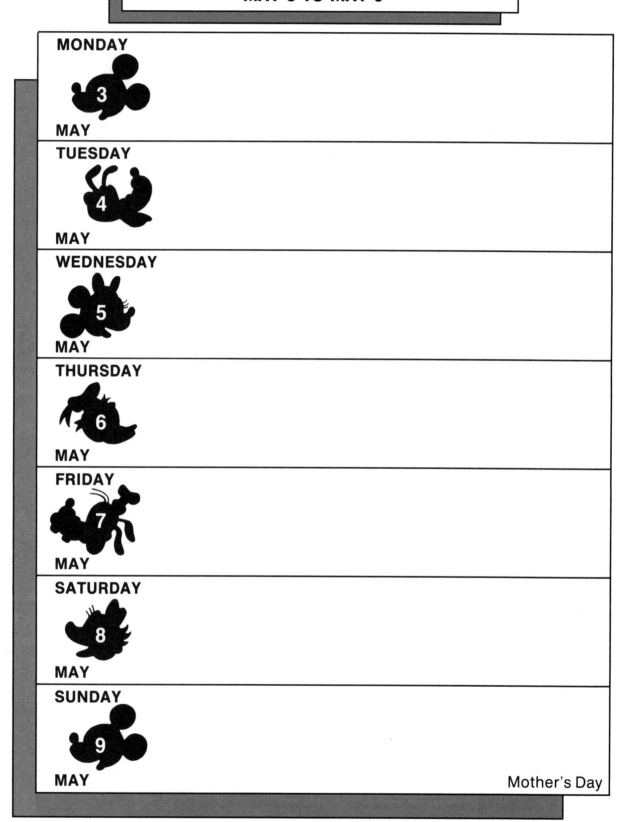

MONDAY

3

MAY

TUESDAY

4

MAY

WEDNESDAY

5

MAY

THURSDAY

6

MAY

FRIDAY

7

MAY

SATURDAY

8

MAY

SUNDAY

9

MAY

Mother's Day

Goof Troop Surprise!

Connect the dots and find out who's on the
end of Max's leash.

MAY 10 TO MAY 16

MONDAY

10

MAY

TUESDAY

11

MAY

WEDNESDAY

12

MAY

THURSDAY

13

MAY

FRIDAY

14

MAY

SATURDAY

15

MAY

SUNDAY

16

MAY

MAY 17 TO MAY 23

MONDAY

17 MAY

TUESDAY

18 MAY

WEDNESDAY

19 MAY

THURSDAY

20 MAY

FRIDAY

21 MAY

SATURDAY

22 MAY

SUNDAY

23 MAY

All Aboard the Merry-Go-Round

    Do you like going around in circles? Would you like to take a horseback ride to nowhere? Just hop aboard a merry-go-round.

    These rides are also known as carousels. In the 1600's, the French used a similar word to describe a pageant where noblemen played games on horseback. In order to train for one of the games, the noblemen built a strange device: They rode on wooden horses that were mounted on beams around a central pole. Servants or live horses pulled the device around the circle. The contraption was so much fun that women and children of the court and even peasants copied it and used it just for enjoyment. Thus the idea for today's carousel, or merry-go-round, was born.

    Eventually steam engines powered the rides. Carousels soon became very popular in parks throughout Europe and North America. In the early 1900's, there were about 3,000 in the United States. Today fewer than 300 carousels still operate. Is there a merry-go-round near you?

MAY 24 TO MAY 30

MONDAY

24

MAY

Victoria Day in Canada

TUESDAY

25

MAY

WEDNESDAY

26

MAY

THURSDAY

27

MAY

FRIDAY

28

MAY

SATURDAY

29

MAY

SUNDAY

30

MAY

JUNE
THE SIXTH MONTH

This lovely month was named for the Roman goddess Juno. She was the patron of women, marriage, and the home. Perhaps that's why so many people get married during June.

June marks the end of spring and the beginning of summer in the northern part of the world. The first day of summer, around the third week of the month, is the longest day of the year. The sun rises earlier and sets later than on any other day. In the southern part of the world, though, winter begins in June.

June is an especially happy month for fathers and children. Fathers look forward to their special day— Father's Day. It's celebrated on the third Sunday of the month. And children look forward to the end of the school term and the beginning of summer vacation. Are you going on a trip? Are you going to camp? Make sure you keep a record of your summer activities in this Diary.

MAY 31 TO JUNE 6

MONDAY

31

MAY   Memorial Day

TUESDAY

1

JUNE

WEDNESDAY

2

JUNE

THURSDAY

3

JUNE

FRIDAY

4

JUNE

SATURDAY

5

JUNE

SUNDAY

6

JUNE

Underwater Colors

Fish that live in tropical waters are among the most colorful creatures in the world. But their colors aren't just for decoration. There are reasons for their dazzling colors and patterns. One is camouflage. Color helps protect a fish from its enemies—for example, colored fish can hide in the colored coral reefs.

A fish's bright colors may also be a warning to enemies that it is poisonous. An octopus that attacks a brilliant red fish and gets stung with poison will remember that fish's pattern and color—and avoid it. Colors also help sea creatures identify others of their kind at mating time. The tropical reef is crowded with different species of creatures. Yet males and females of each species manage to find each other.

Whatever the reasons for these fabulous underwater colors, the result can be summed up in one word: beautiful.

MONDAY

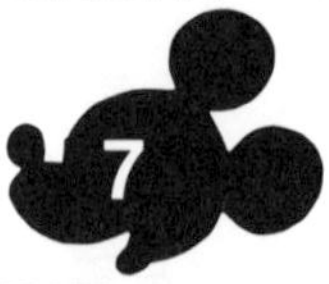

7

JUNE

TUESDAY

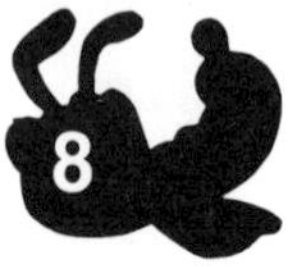

8

JUNE

WEDNESDAY

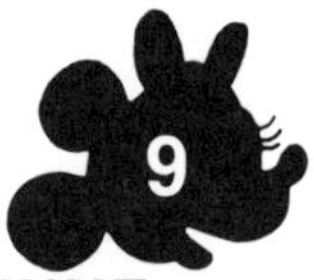

9

JUNE

THURSDAY

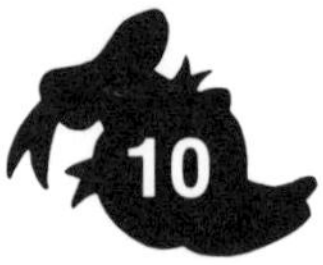

10

JUNE

FRIDAY

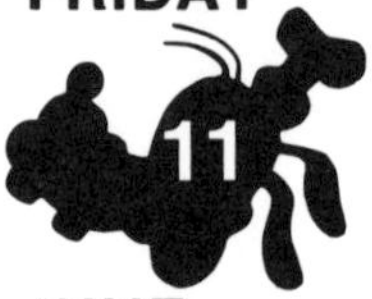

11

JUNE

SATURDAY

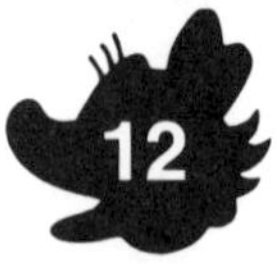

12

JUNE

SUNDAY

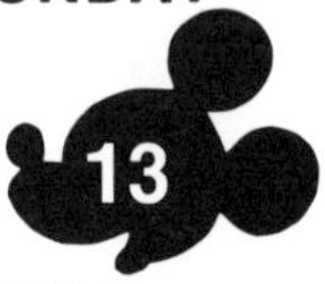

13

JUNE

Children's Day

Hilaire Belloc wrote many humorous poems about animals. This one is about the vulture—and it also gives some good advice on nutrition.

THE VULTURE

The Vulture eats between his meals
    And that's the reason why
He very, very rarely feels
    As well as you and I.

His eye is dull, his head is bald,
    His neck is growing thinner.
Oh! what a lesson for us all
    To only eat at dinner!

JUNE 14 TO JUNE 20

MONDAY
14
JUNE
Flag Day

TUESDAY
15
JUNE

WEDNESDAY
16
JUNE

THURSDAY
17
JUNE

FRIDAY
18
JUNE

SATURDAY
19
JUNE

SUNDAY
20
JUNE
Father's Day

LET'S MAKE MONEY!

Do you need money to go to the movies? To buy a book or a pack of baseball cards? To buy a birthday gift for someone special? There are lots of ways for you to earn money. You can make lemonade and cookies to sell. You can wash cars, rake leaves, or shovel snow. You can grow and sell vegetables or flowers.

Another way to make money—and have fun at the same time—is to have a yard sale. All you have to do is gather up all the items you want to sell. Get your old comic books and magazines, records and tapes, toys, seashells, clothing, and anything else you no longer want. Ask your friends to find some stuff they want to sell and join in. Then put up notices around the neighborhood telling of your sale.

When the big day comes, set up a table outside. Put price tags on the items, and arrange them on the table. Hope your sale is a huge $ucce$$!

Spring Memories

Write down the things you liked best this spring.

My happiest day: _____

My favorite television show: _____

The game I played most often: _____

The friend I had the most fun with: _____

My favorite book: _____

The best trip I took: _____

JUNE 21 TO JUNE 27

MONDAY

21

JUNE

Summer begins in the Northern Hemisphere
Winter begins in the Southern Hemisphere

TUESDAY

22

JUNE

WEDNESDAY

23

JUNE

THURSDAY

24

JUNE

FRIDAY

25

JUNE

SATURDAY

26

JUNE

SUNDAY

27

JUNE

JULY
THE SEVENTH MONTH

Camping. Swimming. Sailing. Traveling. Picnicking. It's time for all these things. It's summer vacation! Well, at least it's summer in the northern half of the world. In Australia and other places in the southern half, it's winter. And there, people are skiing and sledding and building snowmen.

Many countries celebrate their birthdays in July. In the United States, July 4 is Independence Day. This year, the country is 217 years old! This happy day is marked by spectacular fireworks shows and great parades with marching bands.

Other countries also celebrate their independence in July. The Canadian people celebrate Dominion Day on July 1. And on July 14, the people of France celebrate Bastille Day, a holiday that commemorates the French Revolution.

Special Days of Summer

Days I'm looking forward to from July to September:

_____

_____

_____

Birthdays: _____

Holidays: _____

Special days or vacations: _____

_____

JUNE 28 TO JULY 4

MONDAY

28

JUNE

TUESDAY

29

JUNE

WEDNESDAY

30

JUNE

THURSDAY

1

JULY

Dominion Day in Canada

FRIDAY

2

JULY

SATURDAY

3

JULY

SUNDAY

4

JULY

Independence Day

JULY 5 TO JULY 11

MONDAY

5

JULY

TUESDAY

6

JULY

WEDNESDAY

7

JULY

THURSDAY

8

JULY

FRIDAY

9

JULY

SATURDAY

10

JULY

SUNDAY

11

JULY

Your Fantasy Playhouse

What wonderful things would you do if you had your own play-house? Would you play a game of hide-and-seek? Sit and daydream? Read or play games with your friends? Or would you act out an adventure story?

Would you want a playhouse that reminds you of a castle? If so, you could be its king or queen. How about a playhouse that looks like a spaceship? Then you could be an astronaut headed for distant stars. Maybe you would want one that looks like a ship. You could be its captain, guiding it through a stormy sea.

Maybe someday your parents will help you build your very own playhouse. Then you can decorate it so that it becomes your very own fantasy world.

JULY 12 TO JULY 18

MONDAY

12

JULY

TUESDAY

13

JULY

WEDNESDAY

14

JULY

Bastille Day in France

THURSDAY

15

JULY

FRIDAY

16

JULY

SATURDAY

17

JULY

SUNDAY

18

JULY

JULY 19 TO JULY 25

MONDAY

19

JULY

TUESDAY

20

JULY

WEDNESDAY

21

JULY

THURSDAY

22

JULY

FRIDAY

23

JULY

SATURDAY

24

JULY

SUNDAY

25

JULY

AUGUST
THE EIGHTH MONTH

August is HOT! It's beach time. It's pool time. It's mountain time. It's try-to-stay-cool time. Why not spend the last days of your vacation exploring the world of nature? You can watch birds preparing to fly south for the winter. You can keep an eye out for shooting stars that streak across the August night sky. You can spy on chipmunks and squirrels as they dart through the woods, looking for nuts.

Toward the end of the month, start planning for the new school term in September. Do you need pencils and pens? Notebooks? New sneakers for gym?

Apples are ripening on the trees. Harvest time will soon be here. And just as you are planning for school, farmers are planning to sell their crops. Would you like to take a perfect end-of-vacation trip? Go to a farmer's stand along a beautiful country road and buy some delicious fresh corn or tomatoes.

JULY 26 TO AUGUST 1

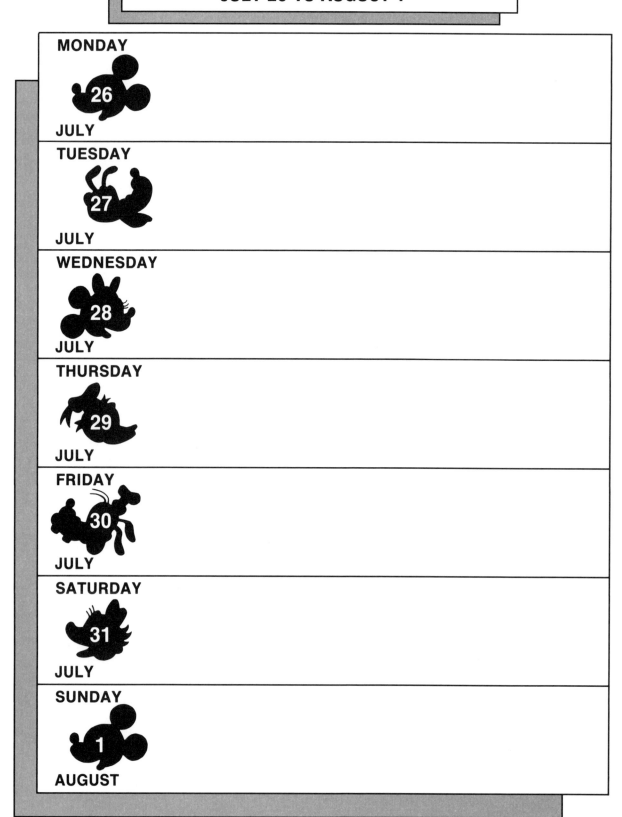

MONDAY
26
JULY

TUESDAY
27
JULY

WEDNESDAY
28
JULY

THURSDAY
29
JULY

FRIDAY
30
JULY

SATURDAY
31
JULY

SUNDAY
1
AUGUST

WHAT HAPPENED TO THE SUN?

On a clear day, we see the sun shining high in the sky. But did you know that sometimes the sun disappears from view—even though the sky is clear blue? This strange, unusual event is called a total solar eclipse.

The word "solar" means "of the sun." And the word "eclipse" means "to hide." In a total solar eclipse, the moon passes in front of the sun and completely hides it from our view. When this happens, the moon blocks the sun's rays and casts a giant shadow on Earth. This type of eclipse usually lasts for just a few minutes.

There are very few total solar eclipses. The last one was on June 30, 1992. There will be only five more during the remaining years of this century. Maybe you'll be lucky enough to see one. But make sure that your teacher or parents help you make a pinhole viewer or get you special dark goggles. Never look directly at the sun during an eclipse —or at any other time. The sun's rays can damage your eyes.

AUGUST 2 TO AUGUST 8

MONDAY

2

AUGUST

TUESDAY

3

AUGUST

WEDNESDAY

4

AUGUST

THURSDAY

5

AUGUST

FRIDAY

6

AUGUST

SATURDAY

7

AUGUST

SUNDAY

8

Clean Room

AUGUST

A PARTY FOR BELLE

There are ten numbers (0–9) hidden in this picture. Can you find them? Put a circle around each number that you find.

AUGUST 9 TO AUGUST 15

MONDAY

9

AUGUST

TUESDAY

10

AUGUST

WEDNESDAY

11

AUGUST

THURSDAY

12

AUGUST

FRIDAY

13

AUGUST

SATURDAY

14

AUGUST

SUNDAY

15

AUGUST

A FLOATING GARDEN

Imagine discovering a beautiful floating garden. It's filled with clusters of round, green leaves, each topped with a colorful flower. Dragonflies dart from blossom to blossom. A frog is using one of the leaves as a small raft. You might not think of a stream or a shallow lake as a garden. But this is where water lilies live.

Water lilies have the same basic parts as flowering land plants. Their leaves, which are called lily pads, are large, flat, and nearly circular. They float on the surface of the water. Water lily flowers come in many colors—white, yellow, pink, blue, apricot, purple.

Perhaps the most spectacular water lily is the royal water lily. Its leaves look like enormous pie plates and may be seven feet in diameter. Even its flowers are giant, growing up to a foot wide.

Would you like to create your own floating garden? Plant water lilies in a pond if you have one, or in small tubs.

AUGUST 16 TO AUGUST 22

MONDAY

16

AUGUST

TUESDAY

17

AUGUST

WEDNESDAY

18

AUGUST

THURSDAY

19

AUGUST

FRIDAY

20

AUGUST

SATURDAY

21

AUGUST

SUNDAY

22

AUGUST

AUGUST 23 TO AUGUST 29

MONDAY

23

AUGUST

TUESDAY

24

AUGUST

WEDNESDAY

25

AUGUST

THURSDAY

26

AUGUST

FRIDAY

27

AUGUST

SATURDAY

28

AUGUST

SUNDAY

29

AUGUST

SEPTEMBER
THE NINTH MONTH

In the northern part of the world, September is the month when summer ends and fall begins. And vacation ends and school begins! You'll see all your school friends again. You can tell them about all the exciting things you did over the summer and find out what they did. What class will you be in this year? Do you know who your teacher will be? What clubs will you join?

The first Monday in September is a special holiday in the United States. It's called Labor Day, and it honors everyone who works. Businesses are closed, and many cities and towns hold parades.

By the end of the month, some trees are shedding their leaves. It's getting a little cooler, and birds are flying south. But the weather can still be beautiful—perfect sweater weather. And it can be windy, too. It's the perfect time to go fly a kite.

AUGUST 30 TO SEPTEMBER 5

MONDAY

30

AUGUST

TUESDAY

31

AUGUST

WEDNESDAY

1

SEPTEMBER

THURSDAY

2

SEPTEMBER

FRIDAY

3

SEPTEMBER

SATURDAY

4

SEPTEMBER

SUNDAY

5

SEPTEMBER

Joke Time

Why can't leopards play hide-and-seek?
Because they are always spotted!

Why did the jelly roll?
Because it saw the apple turnover!

How can you make a witch scratch?
Take away the "w"!

What did the Beaver say to the tree?
It's been nice gnawing you!

WHAT A WHIFF!

Garlic is an herb that's used to flavor foods. If you get a good whiff of it, you'll never forget its strong smell.

Long ago, people thought that garlic had special powers. Athletes ate it to increase their strength. Soldiers ate it to give them courage in battle. Some people even wore garlic around their necks to keep vampires away! And today, it's claimed that garlic helps to prevent heart attacks and other illnesses. Scientists have done little research on garlic, so it's difficult to know if these things are true.

What *is* true is that people eat garlic because they love its strong, unusual flavor. But the herb does make your breath smell terrible! So after eating a garlicky meal, munch on some fresh parsley. This will help you enjoy garlic without chasing your friends away!

MONDAY

6 SEPTEMBER

Labor Day

TUESDAY

7 SEPTEMBER

WEDNESDAY

8 SEPTEMBER

THURSDAY

9 SEPTEMBER

FRIDAY

10 SEPTEMBER

SATURDAY

11 SEPTEMBER

SUNDAY

12 SEPTEMBER

Grandparents' Day

MONDAY

13

SEPTEMBER

TUESDAY

14

SEPTEMBER

WEDNESDAY

15

SEPTEMBER

THURSDAY

16

SEPTEMBER

Rosh Hashanah

FRIDAY

17

SEPTEMBER

SATURDAY

18

SEPTEMBER

SUNDAY

19

SEPTEMBER

SCHOOL DAZE

Pluto went to the head of the class when he named five things found in a schoolroom. What did Pluto name? Unscramble the words and print the letters on the dotted lines. Then put the circled letters together to make another secret word—this word is something every girl and boy studies in school.

sked   ○ __ __ __ __

prape   __ ○ __ __ __

lipnec   __ __ ○ __ ○ __

bloge   ○ __ __ ○ __

lurre   __ __ __ __ ○

Secret Word: __ __ __ __ __ __ __

Answers:
desk, paper, pencil, globe, ruler; reading

Summer Memories

Write down the things you liked best this summer.

The game I played most often: _____

The movie I liked best: _____

The nicest thing I did: _____

The best trip I took: _____

My favorite book: _____

The best new friend I made: _____

My favorite day: _____

_____

_____

_____

MONDAY

20

SEPTEMBER

TUESDAY

21

SEPTEMBER

WEDNESDAY

22

SEPTEMBER

Fall begins in the Northern Hemisphere
Spring begins in the Southern Hemisphere

THURSDAY

23

SEPTEMBER

FRIDAY

24

SEPTEMBER

SATURDAY

25

SEPTEMBER

Yom Kippur

SUNDAY

26

SEPTEMBER

OCTOBER
THE TENTH MONTH

October is a month of change. In the northern half of the world, the days are getting shorter. The weather is brisk and chilly, and plants and animals are getting ready for the coming winter. It's a good time to take a walk through the woods—just to see the trees decked out in their spectacular red and gold fall colors.

Along the way, you might pick up a big orange pumpkin at a farmer's stand. You can take it home and carve it into a grinning jack-o'-lantern. Or you can use it to make a delicious pumpkin pie.

The last day of the month is Halloween! It's a special holiday for children who live in the United States, Canada, Ireland, and Britain. Now is the time to put your new jack-o'-lantern in the window to welcome trick-or-treaters. Are you going to dress up in a costume and go trick-or-treating? What kind of costume will you wear?

Special Days of Fall

Days I'm looking forward to from October to December: _____

_____

_____

Birthdays: _____

Holidays: _____

Special days or vacations: _____

_____

_____

MONDAY

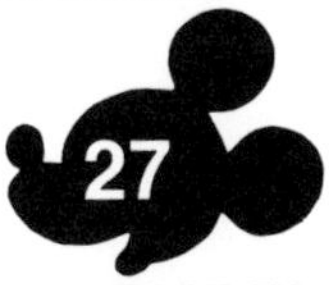

27

SEPTEMBER

TUESDAY

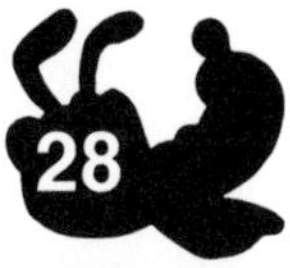

28

SEPTEMBER

WEDNESDAY

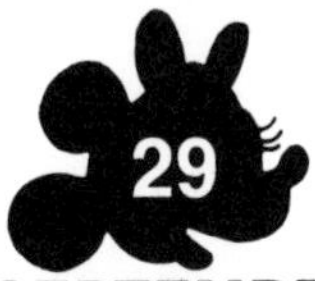

29

SEPTEMBER

THURSDAY

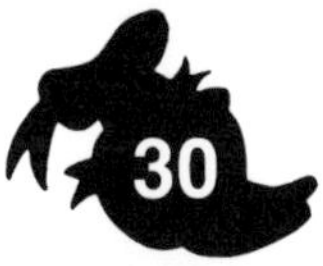

30

SEPTEMBER

FRIDAY

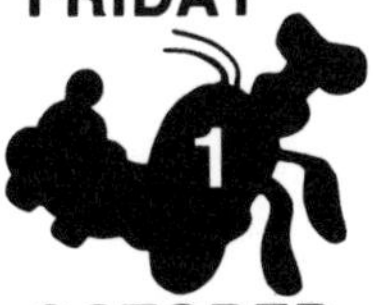

1

OCTOBER

SATURDAY

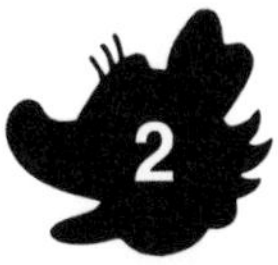

2

OCTOBER

SUNDAY

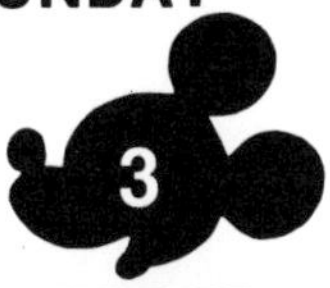

3

OCTOBER

OCTOBER 4 TO OCTOBER 10

MONDAY

4

OCTOBER

TUESDAY

5

OCTOBER

WEDNESDAY

6

OCTOBER

THURSDAY

7

OCTOBER

FRIDAY

8

OCTOBER

SATURDAY

9

OCTOBER

SUNDAY

10

OCTOBER

OCTOBER 11 TO OCTOBER 17

MONDAY
11
OCTOBER

Columbus Day
Thanksgiving Day in Canada

TUESDAY
12
OCTOBER

WEDNESDAY
13
OCTOBER

THURSDAY
14
OCTOBER

FRIDAY
15
OCTOBER

SATURDAY
16
OCTOBER

SUNDAY
17
OCTOBER

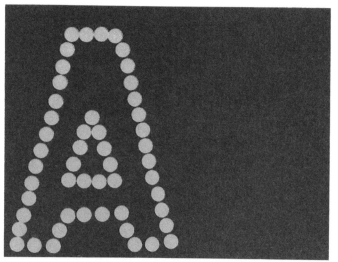

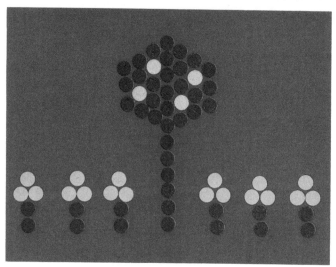

STICKER STATIONERY

It's fun to collect stickers. And it's even more fun to make things with them. You can make your own special stationery or greeting cards. Just take a sheet of white or colored paper and fold it in half. Your message will go on the inside. Use the front side of the paper for your design. You might use stickers to make the initials of your name. Or place a border of stickers around the sheet and do another design in the center.

Some designs using stars and colored dots are shown here. You can copy them, or you can make your own designs. Be creative!

OCTOBER 18 TO OCTOBER 24

MONDAY

18

OCTOBER

TUESDAY

19

OCTOBER

WEDNESDAY

20

OCTOBER

THURSDAY

21

OCTOBER

FRIDAY

22

OCTOBER

SATURDAY

23

OCTOBER

SUNDAY

24

OCTOBER

United Nations Day

OCTOBER 25 TO OCTOBER 31

MONDAY
25
OCTOBER

TUESDAY
26
OCTOBER

WEDNESDAY
27
OCTOBER

THURSDAY
28
OCTOBER

FRIDAY
29
OCTOBER

SATURDAY
30
OCTOBER

SUNDAY
31
OCTOBER

Halloween
Daylight Savings Time ends
(set your clock back one hour)

Dyno-mite DINO-SAURS

Some of them weighed 80 tons and were 60 feet tall. The ground trembled when they walked. They ruled the Earth for 165 million years. Then, 65 million years ago, they died out. These were the dinosaurs, whose very name means "terrible lizard."

But were these beasts really so terrible? Scientists who study dinosaur fossils have recently found that some dinosaurs cared for their young much as birds do. They built nests for them and brought them food. And many dinosaurs traveled in great herds, with older dinosaurs protecting the younger ones.

Other things have also been learned. For instance, it was once thought that all dinosaurs were giants. But in 1986, scientists found the footprints of a dinosaur that was no bigger than a sparrow.

Why did these not-so-terrible lizards of long ago die out? Did the climate turn colder, killing the plants that many dinosaurs fed upon? Did the amount of oxygen in the air decrease? Did a giant asteroid hit Earth? No one knows for sure. But scientists are working on it.

NOVEMBER
THE ELEVENTH MONTH

In the northern half of the world, the days are getting shorter and the nights longer. Cold winds blow. The skies are gray. It's November, and winter's on its way. But in the southern half of the world, it's spring. Summer is coming, and people are getting ready to go on vacation.

On the last Thursday of November, Americans celebrate a special family holiday—Thanksgiving Day. Can you smell the turkey roasting in the oven? Is your mouth watering thinking about the cranberries and sweet potatoes and stuffing? Thanksgiving Day was first celebrated in 1621 by the Pilgrims of New England. When these settlers came to the New World, the Indians helped them plant crops. And after the Pilgrims harvested the crops, they invited the Indians who lived nearby to share the feast. Who will share your Thanksgiving Day dinner? Will your relatives be coming? It's a wonderful time to be with your loved ones.

NOVEMBER 1 TO NOVEMBER 7

MONDAY

1

NOVEMBER

TUESDAY

2

NOVEMBER

Election Day

WEDNESDAY

3

NOVEMBER

THURSDAY

4

NOVEMBER

FRIDAY

5

NOVEMBER

SATURDAY

6

NOVEMBER

SUNDAY

7

NOVEMBER

Clarabelle Makes Music

Clarabelle can play seven instruments! The names of the instruments are hidden in this puzzle. Can you find them? Look in every direction—up, down, forward, backward, diagonally. Circle each word you find. The list below tells you the words to look for.

CELLO   PIANO

DRUMS   TRUMPET

FLUTE   TUBA

HARP

S	H	A	R	P	P	O	D
L	F	O	G	N	L	R	
A	E	L	A	Y	L	U	
B	R	I	U	K	E	M	
U	P	Y	I	T	C	S	
T	R	U	M	P	E	T	

SOLUTION:

NOVEMBER 8 TO NOVEMBER 14

MONDAY
8
NOVEMBER

TUESDAY
9
NOVEMBER

WEDNESDAY
10
NOVEMBER

THURSDAY
11
NOVEMBER

Veterans Day
Remembrance Day in Canada

FRIDAY
12
NOVEMBER

SATURDAY
13
NOVEMBER

SUNDAY
14
NOVEMBER

NOVEMBER 15 TO NOVEMBER 21

MONDAY

15

NOVEMBER

TUESDAY

16

NOVEMBER

WEDNESDAY

17

NOVEMBER

THURSDAY

18

NOVEMBER

FRIDAY

19

NOVEMBER

SATURDAY

20

NOVEMBER

SUNDAY

21

NOVEMBER

A Boxful of Music

Have you ever watched a wind-up toy car race across the floor . . . or a wind-up toy animal do tricks? Wind-up toys are great fun. But music boxes are even more fun. Some of these wind-up devices combine music with action.

The first music boxes were made by Swiss watchmakers in the 1700's. They played only simple tunes. But the ones made in the last hundred years can play the sounds of drums, bells, and sometimes a triangle or gong. And as they play, they often entertain. Wooden children dance around a maypole. Monkeys and acrobats perform tricks. Miniature carousels go round and round. It's almost like watching a music video from the past.

NOVEMBER 22 TO NOVEMBER 28

MONDAY

22

NOVEMBER

TUESDAY

23

NOVEMBER

WEDNESDAY

24

NOVEMBER

THURSDAY

25

NOVEMBER

Thanksgiving Day

FRIDAY

26

NOVEMBER

SATURDAY

27

NOVEMBER

SUNDAY

28

NOVEMBER

DECEMBER
THE TWELFTH MONTH

December is the last month of the year. And what a busy month it always is! Christmas is coming on December 25. Gifts have to be bought. Christmas trees must be decorated. Christmas cards have to be sent. And parties have to be planned.

December may be a busy month, but Christmas makes it a joyous one. Another joyous holiday is Hanukkah, the Jewish Feast of Lights. It's celebrated at about the same time as Christmas and lasts for eight days.

December 31 is the last day of the year. And the night of December 31 is New Year's Eve—the last holiday of 1993. People all over the world celebrate. When the clock strikes midnight, 1993 will be over. Everyone will yell, ''Happy 1994!'' May the New Year bring you and your family health and happiness.

NOVEMBER 29 TO DECEMBER 5

MONDAY

29

NOVEMBER

TUESDAY

30

NOVEMBER

WEDNESDAY

1

DECEMBER

THURSDAY

2

DECEMBER

FRIDAY

3

DECEMBER

SATURDAY

4

DECEMBER

SUNDAY

5

DECEMBER

Walt Disney was born in 1901

What's in a Name?

If you are like most people, you probably have several names: a first name—let's say it's William; a middle name; and a last name, which is also called a family name or surname. Your first and middle names were given to you at birth. But your surname is the same as your parents'.

In China and India, family names go back more than 2,000 years. However, in many Western countries, surnames go back only about 900 years. Many people in the United States have the same surname. Even though there are more than 250 million people in America, there are only about 1 million different last names. So if William's last name is Smith, he's certainly not alone. There are more than 2 million Smiths in the country.

But if William Smith lived in China, he'd probably be the only Smith there. As a matter of fact, he wouldn't even be known as William Smith. His name would be Smith William. The Chinese give their family names ahead of their individual names.

Fall Memories

Write down the things you liked best this fall.

My happiest day: _____

My best new toy: _____

The nicest place I went: _____

My favorite new teacher: _____

My Halloween costume: _____

_____

_____

MONDAY

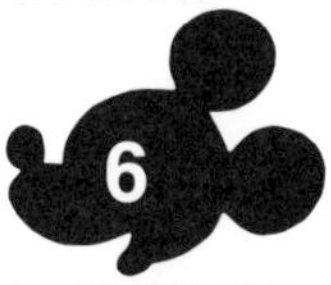

6

DECEMBER

TUESDAY

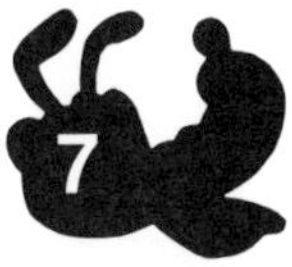

7

DECEMBER

WEDNESDAY

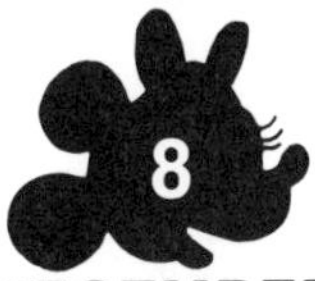

8

DECEMBER

THURSDAY

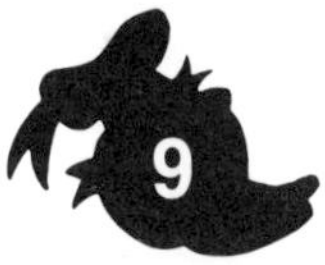

9

DECEMBER

Hanukkah begins

FRIDAY

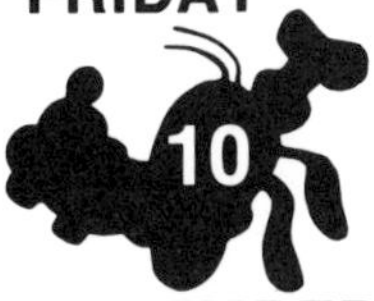

10

DECEMBER

SATURDAY

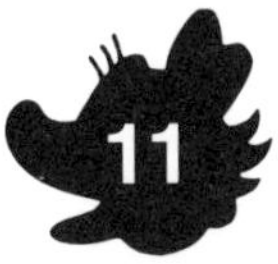

11

DECEMBER

SUNDAY

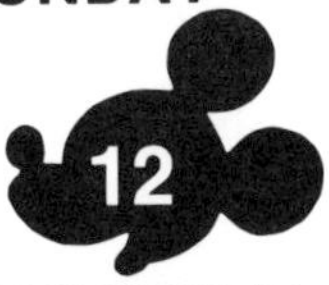

12

DECEMBER

A Letter to Santa

Santa works very hard bringing presents to all the children on his list —and he hardly ever forgets anyone.

But just to be sure, why not write and tell him how good you've been, and remind him of what you'd like to get for Christmas.

_____

_____

_____

_____

_____

_____

_____

_____

_____

DECEMBER 13 TO DECEMBER 19

MONDAY
13
DECEMBER

TUESDAY
14
DECEMBER

WEDNESDAY
15
DECEMBER

THURSDAY
16
DECEMBER

FRIDAY
17
DECEMBER

SATURDAY
18
DECEMBER

SUNDAY
19
DECEMBER

This Is Me

Nearly a year has passed since you described yourself on the THIS IS ME page in January. Have you grown since then? Do you look the same?

Name: _____

Weight: _____

I've gained _____ pounds since January!

Height: _____

I've grown _____ inches since January!

Shoe Size: _____

Shirt Size: _____

Paste a new photo of yourself here. Have you changed since January?

DECEMBER 20 TO DECEMBER 26

MONDAY
20
DECEMBER

TUESDAY
21
DECEMBER

Winter begins in the Northern Hemisphere
Summer begins in the Southern Hemisphere

WEDNESDAY
22
DECEMBER

THURSDAY
23
DECEMBER

FRIDAY
24
DECEMBER

SATURDAY
25
DECEMBER

Christmas

SUNDAY
26
DECEMBER

DECEMBER 27, 1993 TO JANUARY 2, 1994

MONDAY

27
DECEMBER

TUESDAY

28
DECEMBER

WEDNESDAY

29
DECEMBER

THURSDAY

30
DECEMBER

FRIDAY

31
DECEMBER

New Year's Eve

SATURDAY

1
JANUARY

SUNDAY

2
JANUARY

Happy Holidays and New Year's Wishes

As the New Year arrives, and we look back on a happy holiday season, it's time to think of what the months ahead will bring—and to make some New Year's wishes—for you and for everyone in your family.

NEW YEAR'S WISHES

_____

_____

_____

_____

And here's our wish for you:
A happy and healthy
New Year in 1994!